BEGINNING A LIFE WITH JESUS

NEW LIFE

Brandon Goff

NEW LIFE: BEGINNING A LIFE WITH JESUS

Cover and Interior Page design by True Potential, Inc.

ISBN: (Paperback): 9781960024251

ISBN: (e-book): 9781960024268

LCCN:

True Potential, Inc.

PO Box 904, Travelers Rest, SC 29690

www.truepotentialmedia.com

Cover and Interior Page design by True Potential, Inc.

CONTENTS

ACKNOWLEDGMENTS

Thank you to those who see a big call and chase it daily. Megan, my wife - I love you more than words could ever say. You're the most significant support system I could ever imagine. Thank you for sharing life with me.

Brody, Kiley, Cullen - I love you guys! You will grow up and be tremendous world changers. Thank you for making me a daddy.

Mom, Dad, and Eric - Thank you for pushing me to dream, grow, and live for Jesus. I couldn't imagine having a better family. I love you!

Radiate Church staff - you guys are incredible! Thank you for setting the culture and changing the world with me.

Radiate Church - Your passion for Jesus and seeing others live their lives in submission to Him is inspiring. The best is yet to come!

Shaniqua, Thank you for all of your help, support, and encouragement in life and on this project.

Chuck & Stephanie – Destiny friends are hard to come by. Thank you for being that for us.

"PT" – your life may have been cut short on earth, but your impact wasn't. Thank you for chasing vision with me and being a true "swim buddy."

INTRODUCTION

When I was 15 years old, I prayed a prayer at a camp I was attending and gave my life to Jesus, for real. Sure, I'd prayed the prayer before, but this time it was different. This time, I meant it. This time, I would do anything. Well, almost anything. I didn't want to separate myself from my friends. I didn't want to stop partying too much. But I also didn't want to go to Hell. Therefore, I prayed a prayer, and I honestly meant it.

Over the next several years, I lived for God as well as I could. I got it wrong—a lot! But I went to a Christian college, studied to be a youth pastor, and took a full-time youth ministry position at age 20. We had some great success and impact, but I was young and didn't fully understand the extent of the sacrifice needed to follow Jesus.

When Jesus said, "Take up your cross and follow me." I didn't fully get that. So, I got my feelings hurt and walked away from God. He didn't walk away from me, and He didn't give up on me, but I surely did Him.

At age 23, after many medical complications with my heart that caused me to be closer to death than I ever cared to be multiple times, I prayed that prayer of submission and salvation again. Only this time, I was in ICU in a hospital, wondering what the rest of my life would look like, and I meant it. I meant it in a way I didn't mean it before.

This time, I was willing to give up whatever I had to give up. If God wanted me to, I would move to the furthest reaches of the earth and live in seclusion. I had just experienced Him pulling me from an operating table twice; I was in love with His love. I was mesmerized by His grace, mercy, and belief in me. He surely didn't have to give me another chance; after all, I had publicly given up on Him before.

The more I live for God and the more I help people draw closer to Jesus, the more I realize that there are many "basics" that aren't known. People have many questions that need answers and clarification. Some people are extroverts, so they don't have a problem asking. Some people don't want to ask because they don't want to seem like they don't know anything. That's where this book comes into play.

I wrote this book with you in mind, so you could have some of the basic questions answered. Maybe you've heard some things, and you just don't know what to believe or think about what was said. That's why you picked up this book: to gain clarity on what "take up your cross and follow me" really means.

We will answer questions about baptism, prayer, and serving, and even explain who God, Jesus, and the Holy Spirit are. The goal of this book is not to give you something to read quickly. It's meant to be an easy-to-understand guide to the new life you've been given in Jesus. Welcome to your New Life!

WELCOME TO THE FAMILY!

Welcome the family! I'm honestly excited to be your brother. This family is the absolute best group of individuals you can get around. Let me introduce you to a few people.

God, our Father...

Our Father is the best Father around. I don't know what your natural father is like, but I promise God, our Father, is so much better. God loves us so much that He did everything He could to give us an open opportunity to join the family with Him. He knew we would get it wrong, mess up, and screw a lot of things up - but He gave us life and purpose anyway! The amazing thing is that even before we made the decision to recognize Him as our Father, He still loved us.

Honestly, if you're like me, there were times in your life when you weren't even thinking much about

God. Even then, because He's our Father, He loved us! He wanted us to be successful, blessed, loved, and special, even when He didn't like our decisions, our attitudes, our desires. As our Father, He unconditionally loves us, but He will also correct us. Doesn't every loving parent? That's right. He loves us so much that He gave us the opportunity to be in a relationship with Him through Jesus and corrects and guides us with the Holy Spirit and the Bible.

I grew up in a family with high values and expectations. We were expected to use our Southern manners and respond with a "yes/no ma'am/sir," "excuse me," and things like that. If we didn't have our manners, I would be quickly corrected by my parents. I would be given the opportunity to repeat my response, only this time the right way. My parents weren't rude or mean about it, but they were direct about their expectations and what the correct response actually was.

In those moments, I wasn't the happiest kid. I hated being corrected or asked to do something over again. Now that I have my own kids that I hold accountable to values and standards, I understand what my parents were doing. They weren't making a hobby out of correcting me; they were pointing me in a specific direction that they believed was respectful and honoring. I often hear people give God a hard time because of the standards that He holds throughout our lives, scripture, and His teachings.

When we allow God to become our Eternal Father, we submit to His ways and His standards. We are welcoming His loving correction, His tender redirection, and His focus on helping us become the best we can be. He created us with a purpose, a plan, and with love in mind. He knows what's best for us even if we don't like the correction He offers. That is what a loving Father does; He loves us where we are but way too much to leave us there. Welcome to God the Father.

While He loves us where we are, in the midst of our sin, He loves us too much to leave us in it. His loving hand and pure intentions will always point us in the direction of allowing us to walk closer to His love and eternal relationship with Him. That is our Father. That is God.

Jesus, our Savior…

Jesus lived with God in Heaven until God decided sin could keep us from life with Him for eternity in Heaven. At that point, Jesus was sent to Earth as a human, except His mother was a virgin, so she was pregnant with Jesus miraculously. Then He lived a perfect, sinless life for 33 years. He had a very public and powerful ministry from ages 30-33, in which everyone who studied religion and what they had to do to be closer to God found a lot of issues with Jesus' life. They hung Him on a cross to humiliate and kill Him. Here's the kicker in that situation, though: it's what God planned to happen.

I know that can sound really harsh for a loving Father to do, but Jesus had to suffer, hurt, and die on the cross because He was allowing Jesus to die as you and as me. When He hung on the cross, He became our Savior, not because He suffered and died, but because He suffered and died as you and as me. He took our sin, our shortcomings, our pains, and our struggles. He bled for them. He took the verbal punishment, the naked humiliation, and the suffocation on the Cross so that you and I didn't have to.

That didn't end the story, though. No, no, no. Three days after He was laid in a grave to decompose, something miraculous happened. Jesus rose from the dead, found His disciples (followers), and explained to them that He was not defeated. He wanted to show them that He took the death we deserved and that with us on His mind and in His heart, He walked out of the grave so that death and hell don't have to define us!

You and I cannot pay for the separation that sin has offered us. We cannot be our own Savior and our own Redeemer. You and I cannot redeem a relationship between sinful people (us) and the Holy God. Because we cannot do these things, there has to be someone who would step in the gap to pay the debt that we owe but cannot pay. There has to be someone who sees past our muddied life and into our redeemed future with God.

This is where Jesus, our Savior, steps in. Jesus takes on our sin upon Himself and nails them to a sinner's cross. His body was broken so that our souls could be made whole. His blood would pool at the bottom of the cross so that we could be baptized in forgiveness and grace. Jesus decided to become our payment so that we could live free and victorious with Him. Jesus is our Savior, our friend, and our Redeemer!

Holy Spirit, our Comforter...

The Holy Spirit, if I'm honest, is probably the least popular member of our family. He's great! He's helpful and wise, he's comforting and loving, and He empowers us to get better every single time we spend time with Him. The Holy Spirit helps us when we need to be comforted. He guides us when we don't know what to do. He gives us wisdom when we are grasping for straws on how to do things the right way.

The Holy Spirit talks to us personally a lot of times. He speaks through a small whisper in our heads a lot, trying to get us to do something specific or stay away from things we shouldn't be around. He really looks out for us. Not only that, He offers us gifts so that we can have a greater impact on other people. (1 Corinthians 12:8-10). He even gives us something called "fruit" to help us grow stronger with God and help others at the same time (Galatians 5:22-23).

In short, the Holy Spirit is sometimes forgotten because He's more personal. He's within us, and you know as well as I do that sometimes we can get way too familiar with certain things/people and forget to listen to them. I'm encouraging you to listen to Him because he's the direct voice of God. In fact, He is how God connects with us many times.

All three of these, God our Father, Jesus our Savior, and the Holy Spirit our Comforter, work together to make the family of God as loving, welcoming, and renewing as anything you've ever encountered. In this family, you'll meet people that belong to it that you don't look like, sound like, talk like, or really even like, period. But that's quite alright! Just like in any family, it's not our similarities that connect us; it's our blood and our lives. The skin that makes up our bodies and the experiences that make up our lives may all be different, but the blood that runs through our veins has been replaced with the blood that Jesus sacrificed for us to be in this family. And none of us, and I do mean none of us, deserve to be in the family.

As part of the family, we have an "inheritance" that we get to cash in on every single day of our lives. An "inheritance" of love, grace, forgiveness, belief, and eternal life in relationship with King Jesus! Things will still go wrong, be difficult, and hurt us, but now we can handle it because we have a Father, a Savior and King, and the Holy Spirit to comfort us when it hurts more than we expected.

Let me say again: WELCOME TO THE FAMILY! I'm really excited to walk this out with you! Let's talk about a few things that I hope will help you understand a little more about this life-changing decision.

I believe we were all created to do life with others. To walk through life with a circle of people who celebrate, mourn, cry, laugh, and pray with us. We all know these people. My hope and prayer throughout the pages of this book is not just to fill you with information. I truly desire to walk through the base and foundation of your relationship with Jesus with you. I want you to read it more like a conversation at a coffee shop than a book of information. Let's take a little while and do life together.

I hope this book sparks enough thought and interest in your life to make you study, research, and pray through things like you haven't before. Let's dive in, look at our new life with God and others, and see where God takes us.

WELCOME TO YOUR NEW LIFE

So, in the previous chapter, I introduced you to some really important people in your new family. In this chapter, I want to help explain to you what it means that you're in a new life. What it doesn't mean is that your old life was terrible, horrible, and good for nothing. Everything you've been through in your life before giving your life to Jesus has helped develop you into the person you are today. Jesus has "redeemed" your previous life and your previous actions so that you can have a place with Him.

In your new life, you're going to have the privilege of encountering a few things differently. You'll be able to walk in a new life of joy, of love, and of community. Let's dig into each of those together.

Joy

Nehemiah 8:10 says, "For the joy of the Lord is your strength." Nehemiah was a chosen man of God who was sent to rebuild the walls of Jerusalem. The people helping him were getting upset about some outside turmoil and attack, and this was Nehemiah's response. The key to understanding the joy that comes from God is to understand what Nehemiah was saying; the joy from God is our STRENGTH!

When you have Joy from God, it doesn't mean that you never have a bad day, never get sad, and never have a long face. What it does mean is that the joy that comes from our New Life with Jesus is stronger than the sadness that you may have to endure at times. Joy is a mindset, not a feeling. Joy is the ability to look forward to something better than what is going on around you. The thing that gives me strength in my life when I feel weak is being happy that I have a greater outcome on the other side of a difficult situation. I have the greater outcome simply because God has blessed me with it through relationship! Smile. You've got the strength of joy from God!

Difficult days are not exempt from anyone in life. Difficulty is a guarantee in this life, even if we wish it wasn't. In 2023, my best friend lost his life at an incredibly early age. We did everything in life together. He was on staff with me at our church for seven years; our families vacationed together, our kids have grown up together, we celebrated together, cried together, and trusted God together. The days, weeks, and months that followed were not fun, nor were they happy.

In fact, they were dark, difficult, frustrating, and confusing. I questioned a lot, hurt a lot, and smiled a lot less than normal. Truthfully, on the outside, many people who weren't close friends probably wouldn't have noticed much of a difference, but being "happy" was more of a task than it had ever been in my life. During this season in my life, one of the things God taught me in a tangible way is that happiness and joy are not the same thing.

Happiness is an emotion. Happiness is usually an emotion we experience and express when things are going well, and we feel the emotion. Happiness brings a smile and a laugh, induces a lift of adrenaline, and makes us feel "higher." Joy is not an emotion, however. Joy is a choice.

The joy of the Lord is my strength, not because I feel it, but because I choose to focus on the joy, the consistency, the faith, and the foundation of God my Father. I choose to be joyful even when I'm not feeling happy. We can choose to be joyful in our faith and our life with God, even if our life with people is difficult.

Our joy being found in the Lord makes joy a consistent reality even when the emotion of happiness is not. Happiness is dependent on situations in my life. Joy is dependent on my foundation in God. You can experience joy because of the love of God, even if you don't always feel happy. And because of that, joy becomes my strength, even if I feel weak.

Love

There was a very smart man who asked Jesus what was the most important commandment. In those days, "The Law" was a ton of commands and rules that we had to follow. This man knew what they were and wanted Jesus to tell him the fast track to eternal life in Heaven. He wanted to know which was the most important command to accomplish that. Jesus answered in Matthew 22:36-40:

Love the Lord your God with all your heart and with all your soul and with all your mind. This is the first and greatest commandment. And the second is like it: "Love your neighbor as yourself." All the Law and the Prophets hang on these two commandments.

The most important thing you can know about your new life with Jesus is love. First, you must love God. Don't know how to do that? Think about it like a relationship with your spouse/girlfriend/boyfriend. How do you fall deeper in love with them? You get to know them; you know their likes and dislikes. You talk to them a lot; you spend more time with them. The same goes for God; spend time with Him through reading the Bible (His letters to you), worshiping (time in His presence), and praying (hearing Him speak). And the great thing is this: the only reason we can really love Him is that He loves us more! He forgives freely, honors freely, and gives life freely.

The second part of the love you now get to experience is the love for others. To begin with, though, you have to understand that love is not dependent on agreement; it's dependent on commitment. We must commit to loving people no matter their views or choices because God loves them. In this new life, we begin to look and act more like Jesus every second we walk with Him. That means we must learn to see people in the eyes of God, not our own eyes. People will hurt you, wrong you, and make bad decisions. As followers of Jesus, we don't have to agree, but we can still love them! John 13:35 (NASB) says this: "By this everyone will know that you are my disciples, if you love one another."

While we love others regardless of their choices and decisions, it doesn't mean we walk with blind agreement with every choice; it means that we love in spite of disagreement. We live in a world where disagreement is a bad thing. I would contend that disagreement is the real test of real love. It's not difficult to love people you agree with, but it can absolutely be difficult to love those you disagree with. I believe that's why John 13:35 is such a powerful verse. We will be known by the way we live with those we agree and disagree with.

How are we treating other people we encounter in our everyday life? How are we embracing people regardless of disagreement? Are we pointing them to the love of Jesus more than the love of our opinions? All of these are questions that will help us determine if we are loving people like Jesus does. He loves us selflessly, sacrificially, honestly, dangerously, and powerfully. People in this life will know that Jesus is our Savior if we love like He loves.

Loving others like Jesus is completely counter-cultural. It looks, acts, and even sounds different than everyone and everything else in life. Living a life submitted to Jesus Christ looks like something. It looks like radical love. Let's be known by our love.

Community

Community is so important. We were not created to do life alone. We were meant to do life in community with others. That's why belonging to a church is so important and why getting in groups and on teams with others is so key. Community creates accountability and "check yourself" moments. If we don't have community, it's easy to get isolated and stay in the mud and muck of our lives rather than have someone who can add perspective to your situation that you may not see. They can help you learn more than you ever have. I often say this: "Your life rises to the level of your relationships." The reason for that is you'll become what/who you're most closely connected to.

For some of us, it's easier to get into community than others. Some of us are extroverts. It's easy to connect with new people and be in community. For others, it's more difficult since it goes against their personality. The thing about community is that your personality type doesn't matter; it's still vitally important for you to connect. Join a group or class that your church offers, join a team, and begin meeting people on your team. Whatever it takes, community is the secret sauce to authentic relational growth with Jesus and others. You need to know that you are surrounded not only by God but also by others in this new life!

I believe we all need a few levels of friendships and community in our lives. I believe we all need brothers/sisters, mentors, and Pastors. We all need relationships with brothers/sisters with whom we can call and share everything. These are the people we take the mask off, cut loose, laugh, and struggle with. We celebrate with them, cry with them, pray with them, and maybe even yell/scream with them. We have to have some people we can just cut loose and be ourselves without regard.

I also believe we all need mentors in our lives. One of my mentors says that a mentor will ground you to your purpose. A mentor is someone who is ahead of you in a respected area of your life, with whom you have a relationship, and who has agreed to "take you under their wing." They see a purpose and plan in your life and desire to help you become the best you can be. These are people who will ask you the hard and personal questions while calling you up to become better than you are.

Then we all need Pastors in our lives. Pastors are the spiritual guides that help you spiritually navigate your life as you grow. They help you with the deeper theological conversations while helping you learn how to apply biblical principles in everyday life. They are there to help guide you, your family, and your life closer to God and closer to all that He's called you to be.

The beautiful thing about all of these relationships is they can be found and cultivated in the local church. Through Life Groups, through submitting to the Pastor, and through connecting with others. Community is highly important to the growth and maturity of your life and your spirit. I'll repeat something I said in a previous chapter, God didn't intend for us to do life alone. Life is always better connected to God and others!

The new life you've walked into is an exciting example of grace, mercy, and love. You're in a new life because you chose to accept Jesus' forgiveness and because God chose to love you enough to make a way. Your new life is one of constant growth, consistent joy, and authentic community. Let's go!

3

JESUS LOVES YOU TOO MUCH TO LEAVE YOU THERE

We talked a little bit about how your old life wasn't an indictment on you; it was just who you were before you met the life-giving power of Jesus. Now that you're walking in your new life, there's something you need to grasp about Jesus. He loves you entirely too much to leave you where you were or even where you are!

The journey of life with Jesus isn't one of miraculous turnarounds in everything we do. Some of it is a journey. Some of it takes a process, and it takes time for things to turn around. Jesus wants your finances to be blessed, but there may be a process of learning to budget, consistently giving your top 10% (tithe), and paying down the debt that you've accumulated over the years. My point is that Jesus wants to walk with you through all the things He wants to bless and change. He may miraculously change some things in your life because He can, but He may not do it to everything.

The beautiful thing about it being a journey is that it is often where the greatest lessons are learned and internalized. We become who we are by the lessons we learn on the journey of submission and life with our Father, God. And the amazing act of grace is that the journey never ends. As long as you have breath in your lungs, God will walk with you and help you move further down the track of a full life with Him.

John 10:10 says it like this:

"The thief comes only to steal and kill and destroy; *I came that they may have life, and have it abundantly.***"** (NASB, emphasis added)

Jesus proclaims in His own words, and the disciple John records it, that He came to give us life. But, not just a normal, surviving life, a life of abundance! Here's what that means — your life will be a constant journey of growth in every single area of your life as long as you walk and listen to Him. It doesn't mean that you'll get it right all the time and never mess it up. That's a ridiculous thought that many of us have; we *will* mess it up. That's precisely why His love is so astonishing, because He knows we are going to mess it up in this relationship, but His abundant love and life cover us with grace and help us learn from our mistakes, not get lost in them.

Ephesians 1:4 says this about you and me:

"Just as He chose us in Him before the foundation of the world, that we would be holy and blameless before Him. In love." (NASB)

Before the foundations of the world in Genesis 1 were designed and set, you and I were on His mind. He created us all for specific purposes with specific talents and strategic desires. Each thing you have a natural ability for God put within you to accomplish something great for Him so He could use you to show others His love. Some people are great at music, some are artists, some are writers, some are preachers, some are mechanics, some are teachers, and some are great at administration. No matter what your talents or abilities are, the truth is that before the foundations of the world, you were designated to accomplish something powerful for God. Sure, you may never get a microphone on a stage, and you may never have your own television show, but what about the person that you meet in the grocery store or the car rider line? There's your chance!

This is the very reason that I'm convinced that Jesus' goal in His death wasn't about us going to Heaven but about giving us a relationship with the Father and empowering us through the Holy Spirit to bring others on the journey with us. Jesus gave us access to the greatest Father we could ever have a relationship with, so we are loved, empowered, and equipped to be His son or daughter. In other words, Jesus loves us way too much to leave us where we are. He wants us to have a life of abundance. He gave us access, through His death and resurrection, three days later, to have just that!

The resurrection of Jesus, three days after He breathed His last breath on the cross, wasn't just a magical feat that God wanted to blow people away with. It was the opportunity for God to use it to teach us that with our connection to Him, the impossible is always possible! When your dream and purpose seem dead within you, He can resurrect it. When you feel like the life you're living isn't the fullest it can be, He wants you to look back at the empty tomb that was once occupied and know that abundance is the life He gives, not always the life you expect.

Jesus loves us right where we are, but entirely too much to leave us there. And that's a great thing! I don't know about you, but I'm glad I no longer look, talk, act, or live like I did when I was in high school. In high school, I was socially awkward, told and laughed at inappropriate jokes, did stupid things for attention, and thought flirting with a girl I was interested in meant throwing things at her. Now, if I did that, my wife would throw it back and dare me to try it again.

The good thing is that the longer we live life and become students of life, the more we continue to learn and grow. We learn how to adequately carry on a significant conversation. We learn how to, in a life-giving way, build a romantic relationship with the opposite sex if desired. We understand what's appropriate and inappropriate...hopefully. We learn that showing up to work on time is important, and we develop the disciplines that help us be successful at our workplace. The key to these things is simply being able to move forward.

Too often in our spiritual life, the Devil will try to talk us into staying complacent. He doesn't care if we claim we are going to live for Jesus as long as we don't actually do it! It's absolutely impossible for you to live with Jesus each day and stay the same. His very character and nature are that of love, change, growth, and transition. The more we read the Bible, learn from gifted communicators/preachers, and serve Him, the more things change in our lives.

2 Corinthians 5:17 says this:

"Therefore, if anyone is in Christ, he is a new creature; the old things passed away; behold, new things have come." (NASB)

That scripture is important for us to remember because we must know and understand that when we submit our lives to Jesus and relinquish ourselves to the idea that God is our Father, we are not just making a decision. We are not just going on emotions and deciding something because the Pastor asked us to raise our hands. We are literally handing over who we were.

We are handing over our former marriage, our previous porn addictions, and other unhealthy aspects of our old life. We are asking our Father to help us think and develop at a higher level because we can't do it on our own. We are laying our drug addiction at the foot of Jesus' Cross, where His blood dripped down. We are begging Jesus to look at our poor parenting and relationships with our kids with mercy and grace so He can forgive us. We are asking the Holy Spirit to grab our hands each morning to walk with us through life as we mess up and as we celebrate successes.

See, when we become a new creature, the old creature disappears. Sure, you may have some guilt from decisions made before a new life with Jesus. Yes, some of those decisions may have Earthly consequences, but Jesus throws that old "you," that old life, far away and doesn't even see that when He sees you. Psalm 103:12 says it this way:

"As far as the east is from the west, so far has he removed our transgressions from us." (NASB)

Your past is thrown from one end of eternity to the other. It's so removed from who you are that who you were doesn't even compare. Yes, you've gotten it wrong before; we all have. But you've made the decision to give it all to Him, to trust Him, to live for Him. And because of that decision, you no longer have to live where you were; you can now live closer to who He created you to be. Congratulations!

WHAT IS BAPTISM?

We can see a great example of baptism from Jesus Himself in Matthew 3:13- 17. After Jesus was baptized by His cousin, John the Baptist, God's voice from the heavens could be heard as saying, "This is my beloved Son, in whom I am well-pleased." Baptism pleases God because it's an outward example of an inward change that you've experienced.

I'll try to use an example that's easy to understand to illustrate my point. If you clean the inside of your car, you feel great. You throw away all those fast-food cups, take the kid's toys to their room instead of their seats, and you vacuum out the random blades of grass that have made their home in your floor mats. You spend a few hours wiping the dash, getting dust off the gear shift, vacuuming, scrubbing, and even going and getting new air fresheners. It feels great to you and your passengers. You feel a little more proud than you did just a few hours earlier. But in the process, you didn't get to wash the outside of your vehicle. Now you feel great about it, and you know you've made progress, but those not in the car with you can't see the inside, so they can't celebrate with you.

Baptism is showing your family, friends, church family, and anyone else that you're connected to what's happened on the inside. It's a physical representation of the cleaning up and redeeming Jesus has done on the inside. You are committed to it, so you are making it public and open to everyone you know. You're driving around in a shiny, cleaned-up version of yourself, and you want everyone to know it, so you are getting baptized to make it evident to others!

Look at this awesome story in Acts 8:35-38…

Then Philip opened his mouth, and beginning from this scripture he preached Jesus to him. As they went along the road they came to some water, and the eunuch said, "Look! Water! What prevents me from being baptized?" And Philip said, "If you believe with all your heart, you may." And he answered and said, 'I believe that Jesus Christ is the Son of God.' And he ordered the chariot to stop; and they both went down into the water, Philip as well as the eunuch, and he baptized him. (NASB)

This is one of my all-time favorite stories of baptism. The Ethiopian eunuch who is talked about in this story got so excited about the love of Jesus and the internal exchange of an old life to a new life; he just couldn't wait! Baptism is the outward expression of an inward change. Not only is it a physical, external example, but there's something powerful that takes place internally when we walk in obedience of baptism.

Remember back to when Jesus was baptized, and God said He was pleased? Remember, our job is to do all we can to please our God and let Him know our commitment and dedication of our love back to Him. It's not a legalistic act of following rules but a lifestyle of commitment and dedication to Him that does this. Baptism makes God happy! Baptism literally makes God proud of us because He sees we aren't ashamed; we are proud and loud with the new life we've been blessed with.

One of my favorite things about being a Pastor is when I get to baptize people who have committed their lives to Jesus. There's such a power when you see someone go under the water and come back up with that smile on their face. Oftentimes, they will have a hand raised high in the air, a smile on their face, and a peace about their demeanor that comes from the realization that what they just did was life-changing.

I'll never forget the time I got to baptize my two oldest kids. As you can imagine, I was emotional and excited all at the same time. When they expressed their desire to get baptized, we sat them down and explained to them the power of baptism, teaching them much about what is in this chapter. We wanted them to understand that baptism isn't salvation; it's an outward expression of inner salvation from Jesus.

We proudly get baptized because we want to show the life change God has given us.

After those conversations, they agreed they wanted to "take the plunge." I remember when they stepped into that water, and I got to hold their nose and help them under the water and bring them back up. I remember the water dripping off of their faces and the smile that came across the corners of their mouths as they were raised back up out of the water. I remember the brightness in their eyes as their friends and family cheered and shouted in excitement for their decision. And I remember how hard they hugged me with their soaked arms as we cried together in joy at the power of their decision.

Why do I tell you that? Because your decision of baptism isn't just a decision to participate in a church service. You are choosing to show your community where your life is hidden, and that's in Christ. You're making a public declaration that your soul is spoken for by the sacrifice of Jesus and nothing will change that. You are following in the footsteps of Jesus Himself and letting everyone know that God is your Father, and that's how you are now defined.

I encourage you to be like the Ethiopian eunuch and contact your church immediately, find out when the next baptism is, and get your name at the top of the list. When you've done that, go ahead and send invites to anyone you are connected to in your life and invite them to come and celebrate this exciting step of obedience and faith with you. You will never regret it. Baptism is not salvation; baptism is an act of obedience to the salvation and new life we've been gifted!

FIND A COMMUNITY

"Community" in the dictionary is defined as a feeling of fellowship with others because of sharing common attitudes, interests, and goals.

It's important to find a community for you to belong to, and by community, I mean a church. Not just a church that meets on Sundays, but a community of people that meet on Sundays, do life together throughout the week, serve the community they are in, and walk through trials together. The Apostle Paul wrote a great verse in Hebrews 10:24-25 .

And let us consider how to stimulate one another to love and good deeds, not forsaking our own assembling together, as is the habit of some, but encouraging one another; and all the more as you see the day drawing near. (NASB)

Please note the wording in the scripture and how Paul is describing what a life-giving, encouraging, loving community is. A good community has these characteristics: it stimulates one another to do good and gathers together regularly. When we realize that we weren't created to do life alone, finding a good community is a simple concept. We have the opportunity to do life in healthy groups and relationships with others who share a common attitude toward becoming better with Jesus.

When we get involved in a community of people who help us grow, help us do good with others, and help us learn more about Jesus, the one who gave His life for us, it's a lot easier to be the man/woman we are called to be. Make it a consistent, passionate habit to gather with your community. Don't be sporadic in your gathering because going to church on Sundays allows us to allow our pastors or spiritual leaders to speak into our lives. It helps us spend time with others, and it encourages us to serve others without a pretense of who they are or what they do, only what we should do.

Paul pretty much sums it up in the above scripture: gather together, love one another, and serve together. Gather with a church that has a vision you can believe in and support/serve. Gather with a church that supports and loves you where you are but challenges you to go further. Gather with a church that gives you opportunity and grace. Gathering with a community isn't just a Sunday experience, but it's a life-changing, daily opportunity to love!

Let me encourage you to make another decision within yourself about finding a community to belong to. Don't be a consumer in this community; be a contributor. Here's what I mean by that. A consumer is someone who doesn't offer value; they just consume/absorb the product without doing anything to increase the value of it. A contributor is someone who offers value, increases the reach, and makes something better.

Philippians 2:15 says this:

"Go out into the world uncorrupted, a breath of fresh air in this squalid and polluted society." (The Message)

I love this scripture because it clearly states what our purpose is in this world. Our universal purpose is that every person who calls God our Father and Jesus our Savior has the same purpose: to be a breath of fresh air in the world. The only way you can do that is to run from being a consumer and run toward being a contributor.

You can become a contributor in several ways. Here are just a few:

Join A Group

Some churches have Sunday School classes that meet before Sunday morning experiences. Some churches have groups that meet during the week in people's homes or other public places. Both types of groups are designed to accomplish something powerful. They are designed to allow us all to connect with one another in an intimate setting. At our church, we say that this allows us to "do life together." These groups are important for your spiritual journey in many ways.

They allow you to meet people who are living life and struggling just like you are. They allow you to have a group of people to talk to on a regular basis. These groups give you the opportunity to have people who can pray with you and delve into the muck of struggles together. Join a group so you can get to know the people you worship with and have someone to help you with your life!

Acts Chapter 2 lays out a great framework for what it looks like to belong to a local church and even a group of friends that walk through life together. In verse 46 it says that they were "…breaking bread from house to house, they were taking their meals together with gladness and sincerity of heart.". Let's be honest with ourselves here: you don't let people into your house for dinner unless you have a relationship with them. We can deduce from this scripture that the believers were hosting people they had built relationships with for dinner as they grew spiritually together.

Groups are opportunities for us to build relationships with people who go through life just like we do. We all struggle, we all succeed, and we all deal with life differently and sometimes in the exact same way. The key isn't just to go to church but to connect with a group of people who help you become the best you can be. That helps you grow spiritually, emotionally, and in every way possible. If we take our example from Acts chapter 2, it says later in the following chapters that the church was growing daily and people were growing closer to Christ.

Groups help us grow, get better, know more people, and gather around a belief system centered about Jesus Christ. As you are beginning this new relationship with Jesus, I encourage you to find a group that you can belong to. Go bowling together, play golf together, study scripture together, do something together. Just make sure you find a group that looks out for you, points you to Jesus, and helps you become all God has created you to be!

Serve On a Team

There are a multitude of things your church needs your help with. Not because they need another person to do something but because your specific gifts are necessary for that church to accomplish its vision and mission. I talk more about this in another chapter later, but just know that you're needed in your local church!

Pray For Your Leaders

It's easy to fall into the trap of thinking that because they are leaders, they have it all together. That, more often than not, is not true. Leaders have a lot on their shoulders as they must balance family, church responsibilities, and so much more. Pray for the pastor of the church you attend. Pray that God would speak clearly and directly to him/her, not just for great sermons but so that the church would continue to grow and help others grow closer to Jesus, just as you are right now. Pray for your pastor's family, pray for the leaders of each ministry area within the church, and pray for God's blessing over the church as a whole.

If you have found a community in a Bible-based, Jesus-loving, God-fearing, people-gathering church, I can guarantee you that your Pastors/leaders love you and are trying to do all they can to help you grow closer to Jesus. They are studying the Bible to learn more about God so that you can learn more about God. They are praying over you and people you call friends/family. They are asking the Holy Spirit for wisdom on how to handle situations that are breaking the hearts of people that you see each and every Sunday.

Pray for them and with them. Pray for their mind, their marriage, their families, their spirits, and for the church you call home. Ask God how you can be a source of encouragement in their lives as they lead you to the best of their ability. The great thing about prayer is that it impacts the person praying and the person being prayed for. What a magical opportunity it is that we can go before the God of the Universe on behalf of the leaders of the church we call "home."

READ THE BIBLE

The Bible is often, inappropriately, seen as simply a historical account of stories and versions of the same story. This is off base because if it's just a historical account, then there would be no power behind it other than knowledge. What's great is that the Bible is not just a book of knowledge; it's a guide where the words on the page seemingly jump out into the reader's souls and can change something deep within them. The Holy Spirit seems to encompass every word we read and massages it into our souls so that we are not just reading words, but we are living examples of life change with Jesus.

2 Timothy 3:16-17 gives us a great perspective through which we should accurately read the Bible:

All scripture is inspired by God and profitable for teaching, for reproof, for correction, for training in righteousness; so that the man of God may be adequate, equipped for every good work. (NASB)

It's pretty clear here that the Bible isn't just words on a page but that each one is inspected and approved by God Himself. Basically, God spoke through men who were then inspired to write the words we get to read and allow to change our lives. If you want to look a little deeper, God so badly wanted to leave us letters of instruction and inspiration that He left us 66 books of the Bible that were meant just for that! To help, lead, guide, and love us in a deep way.

The Apostle Paul wrote 2 Timothy to his mentee, Timothy so that he could be an amazing leader of the church he was a part of. He said that the word of God, The scriptures as we know them today, were to be considered profitable for teaching, reproof, correction, and training. Profitable means there's a benefit that's larger than when you started at the end of the journey. I find that really amazing because God wants to profit our lives with knowledge, love, joy, and direction. God shows His love for us, as any true father does, by correcting us and helping us see a different perspective.

The Bible isn't something to read just to complete a mindless activity to make God proud of us. The Bible isn't just a journey to be engaged in because behind every story, every family lineage, and every heart shared in the scriptures is a lesson to be learned. We will become better followers of God when we engage in His word. This is a way we can learn of our Father's heart, His character, and His love for the world. This is how we learn how to love others and properly love Him! This is how we lean in and build our relationship with Him at a deeper level.

I like to think of the Bible as our source for the day. Remember the story earlier in this book about the Eunuch's baptism? He told Philip he didn't understand what he was reading. Do you ever feel like that? You have a desire to understand and truly grasp what you are reading because you want to see your life change through it. Here are a few ideas:

Join A Group

I know you're seeing a trend on this one, and I won't write much here, but seriously, joining a group, within your church, helps you have conversations with people who can help you understand much more clearly. You can skip back a chapter and read the idea on this, but groups are life changing, you should try it!

Eat The Elephant One Bite at A Time

If you're just starting to read the Bible, focus on understanding what you're reading more than the amount you're reading. You can read four chapters a day if you want, but if you don't understand a word of it, it will not help grow or change you. However, if you read four verses and you understand them, those verses can impact you deeply and change your life - BOOM! Mission accomplished!

Do not try to grasp and comprehend everything about the Bible within a month. Understand it bite by bite. That doesn't mean that you use this strategy as an excuse to be lazy or undisciplined. Read the Bible daily, but understand what you're reading.

When I was in High School, I had to read *To Kill A Mockingbird*. As with all books to be read in school, we would have reports and tests at the end in order to ensure we understood the overarching theme of what was being taught. Now, I wasn't the best student in the world, but I surely wasn't the worst. I would get my assignments done and usually make a decent grade, but I wasn't doing it far in advance. That would mean that I was reading stacks of pages and chapters a day or two before the report or test.

The main problem with this was that I would accomplish the assignment and usually do well, but I wouldn't learn the lesson. In other words, I was reading for accomplishment but not learning. As I grew up and became dedicated to knowing the scriptures and reading the Bible, this mentality followed me into that. I would read chapters at a time, but I couldn't tell you a thing I had just read. I was great at accomplishing a goal but not learning a lesson.

I heard a phrase one time that I now use in my life regularly. "Don't just read the Bible; let the Bible read you." It's not about how much of the Bible you're reading; it's about what you are learning from the reading. Scripture has the power to transform and change our lives if we allow it to. And it's not from reading it; it's from applying what you're reading.

Here's my suggestion for you as you begin disciplining yourself to read the Bible: don't focus so much on the amount you read; focus on learning from what you read. As you learn from it, you will undoubtedly have a desire to read more and more about the life-giving power and life of Jesus. You will have a passion for learning from the context, culture, and history of what was written, why it was written, and who wrote it while learning what God is teaching us through it.

Follow A Plan

Find a Bible reading plan that you can do. There are "devotions" or plans that go through 2-3 verses a day, and some go through 4-5 chapters a day. Go at your pace, but follow a plan to help you develop the discipline you need to love the Bible. Some plans are topical, so they help you through marriage, dating, finances, forgiveness, love, or other areas of life. Some plans are scripture-based, so they walk you through entire books of the Bible or walk you through the lives of biblical characters. No matter which you choose, choose one, and when that one is over, choose another one.

Here are some places you can find good devotionals to help you:

- Local bookstores
- Download the Bible App from youversion.com
- Your church (Ask your church leadership for recommendations of Bible plans.)
- amazon.com

You can even take a book like this and treat it like a devotional or plan and learn from it. Let the words of the book spur thoughts in your mind and Spirit that then cause you to go learn more about the topic. Read it with a group of people, get together with your group, and discuss it. Check out the videos on our website and let them become an accompanying resource that helps us grow and mature spiritually. The idea is that it's not difficult to lean in to a resource that helps you grow closer to God and with others.

Sometimes, just the thought of reading and studying the Bible can be intimidating. Don't let it be! God left the black and red words that are in the Bible for you to connect with Him. He wants you to read what He left for you and for you to understand it. Nothing that's in the Bible is there by accident or out of place. Every word is there to teach us a lesson and help us progress in this life. Think of it as your playbook for life, much like a football team has a playbook for games. You've got this!

HE WANTS TO TALK

To many new to a life with Jesus, praying may seem like something only older Christians do. Some may think that those who are great at speaking or have been living a life with Jesus longer are the only ones who pray.

The truth is simple: prayer isn't reserved for the best speakers; it's reserved for those who want to have a dialogue with their Father. God longs to hear our voices and feel our hearts. He desires to have us open our ears to listen to Him instead of just our mouths to try to convince Him of our needs.

The first thing about prayer to understand is that it's a dialogue, not a monologue. Prayer is a conversation with the eternal Father of the universe, God. Prayer is a chance that we can hear His voice whisper truth, grace, and love into our hearts. Prayer is an opportunity that, if we take it, God will speak to us more than we speak to Him. Your prayer isn't an opportunity to convince God of anything; it's our opportunity for Him to convince us that He is more than enough.

Don't be afraid or ashamed to pray out loud, either. I'm not talking just about praying in a group of people in your community. I'm talking about when you're by yourself, open your mouth and pray openly. Scientifically, it's been said that when our thoughts exit our mouths, they must first pass through our brains. When our brains process thoughts, they spit out the emotions and desires that accompany words. In other words, what we speak, we become. Openly and proudly declare your prayers.

Prayer isn't just a laundry list of needs and desires that you need from Him, like going to the store. Prayer is a conversation of praise and thanksgiving as well. In the Lord's Prayer (Matthew 6:9-13), Jesus is teaching a group of people how to pray, and He starts by telling them ways to acknowledge God first.

Acknowledge Who He Is

Acknowledge that God is our Father first and foremost. When we talk to other people, we acknowledge whom we are talking to first. We call their name or get their attention in some way so that they know who we are talking to. I believe Jesus asks us to do that, not because God isn't paying attention, but because it positions our heart to receive Him as our Father, not just a gumball machine that we put in a prayer, turn the handle, and an answer falls out.

Make His Name First

It says to acknowledge His name as "hallowed." That means that His name is lifted far and above any other name that you may mention in the prayer. His name is higher than yours, your enemies, your boss', or anyone else you may utter. His name is to be lifted higher because His name is higher than anything or anyone. He can defeat and/or offer more than any other name!

Like I said earlier, prayer is not a list of things that we need; it's an opportunity to talk with our eternal Father. It's not just an opportunity to talk to Him, but for Him to talk to us. He can help us understand His will, His heart, His desires, and His direction, not just ours. Prayer is a direct connection to the Father that has given us a life that we should be honored to live. That doesn't mean that you never tell Him what you need/want in life. In fact, I believe He likes it when we do, but we can't make that the heart and soul of our prayers.

Psalm 37:4 says this:

"Take delight in the Lord; and He will give you the desires of your heart." (NASB)

This is the scripture that is often misunderstood and what can cause us to make our prayers to God a wish list. The order of the words in this verse is imperative to understanding what prayer is.

The above verse tells us that if we first take delight in the Lord, then He will give us the desires of our hearts. Here's what that literally means. It means that we must delight in Him first because when we delight in Him, our heart gets on the same page as His heart, which means what He desires, we desire.

Let's think of it from a child's perspective. I have three kids, two of whom, at the time of this writing, are old enough to play sports and make their own decisions. One is less than a year old, so he hasn't begun this phase yet. Kids would be perfectly fine in life if we just let them eat brownies, drink Mountain Dew, and never take baths or brush their teeth. Their desire is to be loose cannons with little discipline. It's the natural, human way. I guess they are just trying to get back to our caveman lineage.

Now, as the parent, we know and understand that can't be the case. They can't eat brownies and drink Mountain Dew at all because they are way too energetic as it is, and that will just make it worse. That'd be like giving the Tasmanian Devil an IV of caffeine. They have to take baths and brush their teeth because not doing so is unhealthy for them. It's not just that it helps them not stink and helps them look decent. It literally improves their health and sustainability.

Get this: their desire is to do one thing, but our direction is to do something else. When our little ones get older and start to understand our why and our heart behind why they must do these things, their desires will change. Some of you out there may have teenagers who want to take three showers a day. Some of you may have kids who are health conscious, so they eat healthy. That's a great thing. Over time, their desires shifted to meet your desires because they began to understand the importance of what you have been teaching them.

The same thing happens as we begin to take steps to grow with God; our desires shift toward his desires for us because we understand His why much better as we begin to take steps to grow with God. The more we read and study the Bible, the more we talk to God, worship Him, discuss Him in our groups, and tell others about how we came to know him and how they can, too. In other words, our desires become His desires because we delight in the Lord more than ourselves.

When I began dating my wife, I took notice of the kind of cologne she liked me to wear. I paid attention to the kind of clothes she liked for me to wear and how she liked my hair. Do you know why I cared? Because I delighted in her company. I enjoyed being around her; I was delighted that someone like her thought I was attractive in any way at all. Seeing her joy in my efforts, her desires became my desires, and I operated in them. Because of that, her desires became my desires, and I operated in those desires.

I want to encourage you to talk *with* God in prayer, not just *to* Him. Have a conversation. Listen as He talks back. God can speak to each of us in different ways. Delight in the fact that the Father of the universe and all mankind is taking time to be with you. Take delight in the fact that He loves you so much that He gave you a path to restoring a relationship with Him, a path through Jesus. Delight in Him, and your desires will eventually match His. It's a glorious day when that begins to happen!

Hebrews 4:16 says that "...we can approach the throne of God with confidence". When we pray, we are approaching the throne of God with the confidence that we know that He is our Father and wants to hear from us. We are also able to approach with the confidence that we need His grace and mercy in our lives, and He gladly gives us access to them through His throne and love. What an honor and opportunity we have to boldly and confidently enter God's presence through prayer and spend time talking to the creator of the universe!

Prayer isn't designed to change God's mind but for God to change our hearts. The more time we spend with Him, the more our hearts, desires, passions, and attitudes will look different. I like to often say, "Nothing eternal happens without prayer." When we spend time with God in prayer, we are spending time with the author of Heaven and Earth, time and space, eternity, and mortality. What a chance it is for eternity to forever be altered in lives simply by spending time with God.

GET INVOLVED

Earlier in this book, we discussed that through your decision to start a new life with Jesus, you have been given access to specific purposes and abilities. That's true for everyone that is reading this book today. It doesn't matter what your past looks like, what your profession is, or what is happening in your life at this exact moment. You have a purpose and ability to help further the Kingdom of God in the Earth!

One thing I believe every follower of Jesus should do is serve in their community or local church and serve others. The local church you are committed to should have many opportunities for you to serve during the week or each Sunday. Find what opportunities excite you, make you jump with joy, or make you smile when you think about them. Pray about it and ask God to tell you what area you should be using your abilities in. There are a few things about serving that you should know from the beginning.

Serving Is Growth

If you read the life and ministry of Jesus in Matthew, Mark, Luke, and John, you will see that the disciples who walked with Jesus daily served others with Him. Jesus served others just as much, probably more than the disciples. Serving others for the love of Jesus is growth. Serving helps you grow because it helps you get to know others, it helps you respect what others are going through, and it causes you to get involved in the work that God is doing in your church.

What an opportunity God has given us when we have the chance to use our abilities and talents to help others experience the life-giving love of Jesus. The talents and abilities we have been given are God's gift to us; what we do with those talents and abilities is our gift back to God. It's a humbling reality that God chooses to invite us to partner with Him to use our abilities to help others experience His love and grace as we have.

Using those abilities allows us to become better at them. If God thinks enough of us to give us these abilities, it should be our priority to use them and become great with them. Find a ministry at your church and get involved. Wherever you enjoy serving, you're gifted at serving, and there is a need; fill that need and help them reach people for Jesus!

Serving also allows you to make your community even better than it was. It's our way of adding value, in a practical and spiritual way, to the community that we get to call home. When we partner with the local community to serve those who are facing food scarcity, help the homeless find shelter, or clean the ditches along the road – whatever it is we do to serve our community, we do it for God and watch Him use it for His glory. This is our chance to show a practical love of God like few have ever seen!

Serving Comes Before Leading

Before you can lead anything, you have to learn how to serve first. Serving is the heart of Jesus. No matter what, don't expect to be a leader of a ministry immediately. You may have the gift of becoming a leader, but don't expect to become one quickly; instead, serve with others. Serve the needs of other leaders and help people meet Jesus before expecting to be a leader. Jesus loves to promote people with the heart of serving rather than the heart for being seen. Serving others can create a posture of learning and humility more than anything else on the planet.

Without people, the Church cannot do everything God has called the Church to do. It takes people assisting the leaders of the Church, the pastors, and all the people in the community in order for the Church you belong to be effective. As a Pastor, I can assure you that it's impossible for us to do what we know should be done by ourselves. And the great thing is that God knew this from the beginning, which is why He gave each of us different talents and abilities.

God's desire for our lives is to do everything we can to ensure that His Kingdom is spread throughout the Earth. That requires action and movement on our part. That requires us to serve. You know as well as I do that one of the greatest ways to show others we love them and believe in them is to serve them. Join a team, serve the team, worship God while doing it, and watch yourself grow incredibly!

Serving is less about what you do and more about who you do it for. What I mean is that serving is a selfless endeavor that requires us to care less about our desires and more about the potential within others. We serve our local church because it creates a place where others can come learn about how good God is. We serve others by helping elderly people at the grocery store, moving a shopping cart for an expectant mother, and praying for a terrified teenager because these acts create a moment where God can be glorified.

9

DON'T KEEP IT TO YOURSELF

One of the worst things you can do with your new life with Jesus is keep it to yourself. Go out and tell the world about your new life! Tell them how excited you are, how you've changed, and how forgiving Jesus is. Sure, some people won't understand, and some won't believe you, but just keep living it out and let your life speak for you.

Remember that your past doesn't define you, but some people will try to make it define you. Some people who know who you were and what you did may remind you of that way too often because they don't understand that you've submitted your life to Jesus, and they want the old you back. You can't go back to the old you because you're now a new creation!

While there may be times when old desires try to creep in, you are a new creation with a new knowledge of Christ. You'll never be able to live that old life again because that person doesn't exist anymore.

The new you wouldn't feel the same about giving in to those old desires as they did before. You're living a new life!

Don't let that discourage you, though. Invite people to church with you on a regular basis. Think about it like this... if you hadn't shown up, you might not know what it means to give your life to Jesus, belong to a loving community, and serve an awesome Church. Let them experience the same life-changing things you continue to experience.

Tell people your story whenever you get a chance. One of the things the devil will try to convince you of is that your story isn't beneficial, and no one needs to know it. The reason for that is that he knows that stories encompass people's attention. If you tell your story to someone who may be struggling with the same things and then tell them how Jesus loves you and changed your life, they may give their lives to Jesus, too. There's a God out there who loves you and believes in you. There's a church that loves and encourages you, too.

Once you've begun a new life with Jesus, your greatest responsibility is to help others start their new life with Him as well. I like to say it like this: we are responsible for bringing as many people as possible on the journey with us. Wouldn't it be amazing to get to Heaven and see our friends and family up there with us? Your new life is an exciting journey for you, and it could be an exciting journey for others as well.

Let your life speak of your change as well as your words. Telling your story is important, but it's also vital that you let them see your growth through how you live. Your actions and reactions will be changing soon. Your attitudes will be shifting soon as well. You'll even notice some of your habits begin to change. Not because you feel guilty but simply because you know you are loved and you love God back. Don't be ashamed to let others see that; in fact, invite them in to see the changes in your life. Don't keep it to yourself!

I want to use an old story to help you understand the importance of sharing the life-giving love of Jesus with everyone you can.

Imagine a child with an incurable disease. The child had been taken to the best doctors. The best their family could afford—and ones they couldn't. All of these doctors agree on the original diagnoses and that the child could not be cured.

That is until the parent talks with the last doctor on their list. The doctor told the parents about a cure that had just become known to the medical community, yet it was difficult to obtain. In fact, their child isn't the only child who has been diagnosed with this disease. It is more rampant now than it was a couple of months ago. Surely, they'd want this treatment for their child, but would they tell anyone else?

The answer from them and from us is a resounding "YES!" Of course, we would tell others. We would make social media posts, pay for billboards, make phone calls and texts, and do all we could to ensure that people got to the place where they knew there was a cure. Can I be frank with you for a moment?

That is a story of lesser importance than the one of our spiritual lives.

Our friends, family, neighbors, kids, and strangers are dying all around us from an incurable disease known as sin. Sin is whatever creates a divide from the loving arms of our Father God. It's the things that keep us from surrendering and submitting our lives to the life-giving love of Jesus Christ. They are dying of the disease known as sin every single day of our lives. And we have the opportunity to share about a cure that's actually easily obtained.

Sure, we must give up everything in order to obtain Him, but we gain life, forgiveness, grace, love, mercy, purpose, promise, and so much more. We inherit a new family that blows us away and embraces us with purpose! Don't hold this newfound love and grace to yourself. Don't you dare allow this to burn on the inside with passion and fire for a month and then slowly fizzle out with the worries of the world.

No! You hold on to the love of the Father God, the sacrifice of the Savior Jesus, and the direction of the Holy Spirit. You let that drive you, push you, and propel you day in and day out. Refuse to let the disease take over in your life. Refuse to let yourself watch others die of a disease you know the cure to. Because here's the truth: you and I are chosen to be the very advocates that the Father can use to share the cure with everyone else. We are His voice! We are His people! We are His chosen! And know that a community of believers is there to help when life gets tough. Let's go live this new life together!

ABOUT THE AUTHOR

Brandon Goff is the pastor of Radiate Church in Columbia, South Carolina, and the current Executive Director of the Acts 2 Network.

Brandon and his wife, Megan, planted Radiate Church in 2012 with the purpose of equipping and empowering people to impact their communities with the love of Jesus. During his time as pastor, Brandon has seen physical healings, over 500 salvations, several hundred baptisms, a booming kids ministry, and incredible spiritual and numerical growth. The church began with four people in a 20 x 20 room. The church purchased its first permanent facility in December of 2020, during the COVID-19 pandemic, and is now a two location church ministering to around 750 people weekly. The philosophy of ministry at Radiate Church is built around developing leaders, active followers of Jesus, and individuals who live their God-given purpose on this earth - to make a difference - day in and day out.

Brandon had to have a pacemaker at age 23 due to a heart condition and complications during surgery. He has had over ten heart surgeries and has been told three times that he should never have left the operating room alive. His drive in ministry is to make the most of every day, a philosophy birthed from his medical history and personal experience of how God has saved his life spiritually and physically.

Brandon and Megan have three amazing kids: Brody, Kiley, and Cullen.

You can reach out to Brandon at: http://www.brandondgoff.com/

or on:

Facebook:
https://www.facebook.com/bdgoff/about

Instagram:
https://www.instagram.com/pastorbgoff/

YouTube:
https://www.youtube.com/@RadiateChurch

Twitter/X:
https://twitter.com/pastorbgoff